#Relationship Goals

An adult coloring/activity workbook intended for singles and couples to build towards healthy relationship goals.

Nichelle Mitchell

Relationship Goals

by Nichelle Mitchell

Copyright © 2021 by Nichelle Mitchell.
All rights reserved.
Published by THE BOMBCHELLE LIFE Co.

This book was created and designed by Nichelle Mitchell.

Illustrations created by:
Nichelle Mitchell, Faisal & Jerron Couture

No portion of this book may be reproduced, copied, scanned, or distributed in any printed or electronic form without permission from THE BOMBCHELLE LIFE Co. Brief quotations are permitted in book reviews or social media platforms.

ISBN: 978-0-69204-031-7

For more, visit: www.bombchellelife.com

Dedication

This book is dedicated to all the beautiful souls in the world. To all the amazing humans that choose to spread love instead of negativity. Continue to spread that love because the world needs more of that.

To my lovely parents, Arthur and Marion Mitchell...
Thank you for being the ultimate relationship goals and best parents you could be. I am thankful to be able to grow up witnessing such authentic love and compassion. Thank you for teaching me to honor and respect others and more importantly, respect myself. Your marriage is truly admirable and something I look forward to in my future.

To my dear sisters,
Thank you for being my rock, my best friends and my shoulder to lean on. Having you three as my sisters, I know that I have true friends for life.

To my brother,
Thank you for being my hype man and protector.

To my beautiful and brilliant children,
You are my entire universe, motivation and strength. Without you two my world would be incomplete. I love you all beyond words!

To everyone that follows me and supports me... THANK YOU!

And above all, thank you, Jah, for giving me the strength and will to never give up on myself and for always building me back up every time I think that I can't.

 I am thankful,
I am grateful,
I am blessed.

This Book belongs to:

_____

Date: _____

Introduction

Dear Ladies and Gentlemen!

If you are reading this right now, I would like to say thank you and I hope this book brings some value to your life. I was inspired to create this Relationship Goals Coloring/Workbook after my own share and personal experience with relationships - both good and bad.

I can now proudly say that I overcame a lot of heartache and pain and I didn't allow that to break me or make me into a bitter person. I decided to turn my pain into power and put it towards something positive that can help others that may have experienced the same thing as me. These lessons have only made me a stronger and wiser woman.

Please understand that no one is perfect and no relationship is perfect. There will be many ups and downs. However, there are some things you should never accept no matter how much you believe that you love someone. On Social Media I often see people idolizing toxic relationships and basing relationship goals off of popularity and materialistic things that they see. This is another reason why I created this book. I want to provide a different and more realistic perspective to the younger generation. I want people to know that relationships are more than posting cute pictures together or owning nice things. By no means am I a relationship expert and I don't intend on becoming one but I thought I'd create this book to inspire singles and couples to build towards more healthy relationship goals based off what I learned through my experience and from other healthy relationships and marriages that I've been surrounded by.

I want this book to be fun but in the same time helpful for those that put use to it. I hope that with this book I'm able to inspire as many people as possible to know their worth, value themselves more, value others more and spread more love and joy.

Now grab some pens and coloring pencils and dive into this book. There is something for everyone and I hope you will enjoy page after page.

Thank you for your support!

Author,
Nichelle Mitchell

thebombchellelife.com

Love

Is patient, love is kind. It does not envy,
it does not boast,
it is not proud.
It does not dishonor others,
it is not self-seeking,
it is not easily angered,
it keeps no record of wrongs.
Love does not delight in evil but rejoices
with the truth.
It always protects, always trusts, always hopes,
always perseveres,
LOVE never FAILS.

1 Corinthians 13: 4-8

Self Love

"Self love is not selfish; you cannot truly love another person until you know how to love yourself."

What does self love mean to you?
_____
_____

When do you feel most confident?
_____
_____

List 10 things you love about yourself:

_____	_____
_____	_____
_____	_____
_____	_____
_____	_____

What are you most proud of? (About yourself)
_____

Name 10 things you can do to start taking better care of yourself:

_____	_____
_____	_____
_____	_____
_____	_____
_____	_____

Self love means realizing that you need yourself more than you need anyone else.

Your relationship with God will set the tone for every other relationship in your life. Put him first and watch how your life change for the better.
Trust in him!

Self Love

"Happiness starts with you. Not with a man, not with a woman, not with your job, not with your friends, not with money, but with YOU!"

What do you need to start living a happier and richer life?
_____
_____

What can you do to show yourself more love and care?
_____
_____

What would you do if you weren't afraid of failing?
_____
_____

What or who do you need to let go of to become happier?
_____
_____
_____

Name 10 things you do for personal development and growth:

_____   _____
_____   _____
_____   _____
_____   _____
_____   _____

PS. Love the shit out of yourself because YOU matter!

Love Affirmations

The universe is rooting for you. Repeat these affirmations daily to bring positive energy into your future or current relationship.

- I attract positive and healthy relationships
- I am worthy of love and romance
- There is love all around me
- God will bring the right man/woman into my life
- I attract lasting relationships in my life
- I let go of all negativity that rests in my body and mind
- My soulmate loves me above all others
- My partner believes in me and loves me unconditionally
- My future partner will be my best friend
- I welcome a supportive and faithful partner
- I choose to love myself before I love anyone else
- I have respect for myself
- I release all fear and open my heart to love
- I am grateful for the ability to love and be loved back
- I feel safe with my partner

"Don't pray for love. Pray that you'll be ready for love when it introduces itself to you. Pray that its real. Pray that it's unconditional. Pray that it lasts."

Repeat daily:

IT'S OKAY TO LOVE MYSELF

IT'S OKAY TO LOVE MYSELF

IT'S OKAY TO LOVE MYSELF

IT'S OKAY TO LOVE MYSELF

IT'S OKAY TO LOVE MYSELF

IT'S OKAY TO LOVE MYSELF

IT'S OKAY TO LOVE MYSELF

IT'S OKAY TO LOVE MYSELF

IT'S OKAY TO LOVE MYSELF

IT'S OKAY TO LOVE MYSELF

IT'S OKAY TO LOVE MYSELF

What do I bring to the table?
LOVE IS A TWO WAY STREET!

List all your relationship traits you feel can add value to your future or current partner.

_____
_____
_____
_____
_____
_____
_____
_____
_____
_____
_____
_____
_____
_____
_____
_____
_____
_____
_____
_____

What are you seeking?

List below some of your must have standards and requirements that you seek in a relationship.

_____
_____
_____
_____
_____
_____
_____
_____
_____
_____
_____
_____
_____
_____
_____
_____
_____

Everyone should have standards and certain requirements that you seek in a relationship. But do not have expectations! Expectations can lead to disappointments which can lead to heartbreak.

Joshua 1: 9

Be STRONG and COURAGEOUS. Do not be afraid; do not be discouraged. For the Lord your God will be with you wherever you go.

No more unhealthy attachments!

Write about your Personality

and what personality traits do you look for in others?

"When people show you who you are, believe them."

- Maya Angelou

Love Letter to bae

Write a love letter to your bae expressing how you feel about him or her. Recap on a special day you spent together and explain why it was so special. If you're single write about how you would like your future partner to make you feel.

Dear:

Date:

Do you believe ...

that once a cheater is always a cheater? Explain your answer.

_____
_____
_____
_____
_____
_____
_____
_____
_____
_____
_____
_____
_____
_____
_____
_____
_____
_____

"When someone shows you who they are,
believe them the first time."
- *Maya Angelou*

Are you afraid to love again?

Explain why or why not:

_____
_____
_____
_____
_____
_____
_____
_____
_____
_____
_____
_____
_____
_____
_____
_____
_____

> "The bravest thing you will ever do
> is love again."
> *- Madalyn Beck*

What is worse?

In the following space below explain your answer. What is worse: Never trying or trying but failing many times?

If you can love
the wrong person
so much, just imagine
how much you can love
the right one.

What are you tolerating?

Go into detail and jot down the things that you are currently tolerating. Don't be afraid to be completely open and honest with yourself. Explain why you're tolerating these things and if it's worth it or not.

"Your soul mate exists. Soul mates must often go through many challenges before they can find each other."

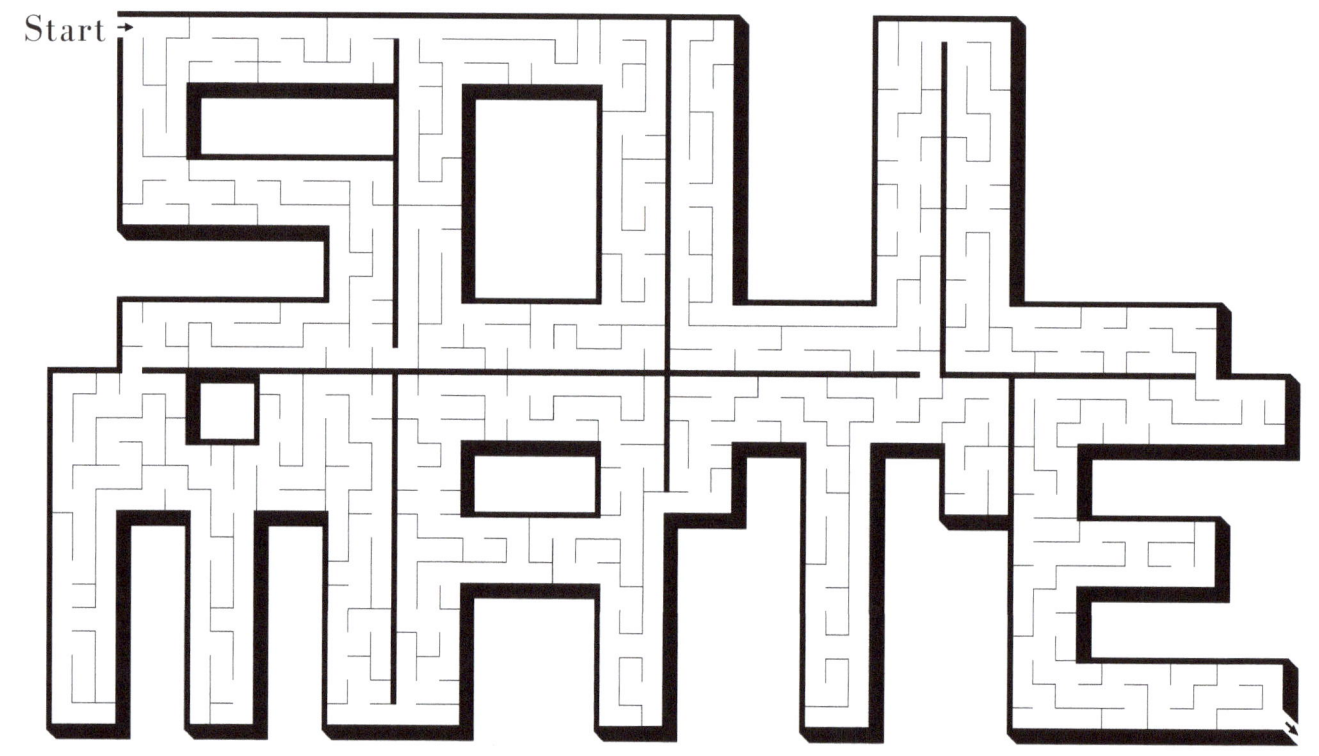

Start

Complete

Key: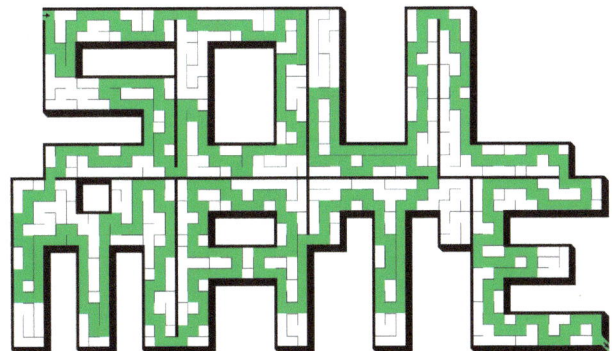

About my Soulmate

Use the section below to describe your current/future soulmate:

_____
_____
_____
_____
_____
_____
_____
_____
_____
_____
_____
_____
_____
_____
_____
_____
_____
_____
_____
_____

Soulmate definition:
1. A person who is perfectly suited to another in temperament.
2. A person who strongly resembles another in attitude or beliefs

Relationship Vision Board

Draw or paste your relationship goals below:

Name:	Partner:
Date:	Future Marriage Date:

Use this space to freely express yourself without fear, disapproval or criticism. Post exactly what you want to manifest in your future relationship/marriage.

Relationship

Performance Report Card

Feel free to make a copy of this page and use quarterly to track improvements.

Partner´s Name:

Graded by:

Final Grade:

Date:

Relationship Categories | Grade Evaluation

Relationship Categories	Grade Evaluation
1. Communication skills	
2. Quality time	
3. Love and affection	
4. Honesty, trust and loyalty	
5. Contributes financially towards bills/dates	
6. Attitude and behavior	
7. Compliments and encouragement	
8. Bedroom activities	
9. Romance	
10. Spontaneous/optimistic	

Grading Scale

O* = Excellent
O = Outstanding
VS = Very satisfying
S = Satisfying
NI = Needs Improvement
F = Failure

Additional comments:

His & Her needs

His needs	Her needs
1. Love	1. Love and Affection
2. Recreational Companionship	2. Conversation and Attention
3. Praise and Admiration	3. Family dedication
4. Encouragement	4. Initiation
5. Support	5. Honesty
6. Respect	6. Quality Time
7. Attractive Spouse	7. Financial Support
8. To feel wanted	8. Loyalty/Trust
9. Sexual fulfillment	9. Security
10. Acts of service	10. Respect

Ice Breaker Questions

Dating can be super awkward, especially if it has been a while since you have been on a date. Here are some ice breaker questions that can spark up a conversation and break the ice.

- What would you do if you knew you wouldn't fail?
- How would you describe yourself using only 3 words?
- What do you enjoy doing most?
- If you had to choose only one food to eat for the rest of your life, what would it be?
- If you could choose a famous actor or actress to play your life in a movie role, who would it be?
- When was the last time that you tried something new and what was it?
- What gets you excited about life?
- What was your greatest life moment so far?
- What is your favorite thing to do?
- What is your biggest pet peeve?
- Do you have any special or weird talents?
- Who is your favorite music artist?
- Do you believe in soulmates?
- If you were the opposite sex for one day, what is the first thing that you would do?
- What do you find most attractive in a man/woman?
- Have you ever been in love?
- Do you want to have or do you have children?
- What do you love most about yourself?
- What was the last thing you've done to help someone else?
- Do you prefer indoor or outdoor activities?
- What is your favorite memory?
- Are you an optimistic person?
- What is your biggest fear and why are you afraid of it?

RELATIONSHIP RULE:

If your partner would question it, be hurt by it, be offended by it, be embarrassed by it, or angered by it, DON'T DO IT.

Relationship Building

As a couple our greatest strengths are:

My partner makes me happy by:

Things we have in common:

Some places we would like to visit:

Our 5 Future Goals:

1.
2.
3.
4.
5.

30 Day Relationship Challenge

Together take 30 days to rekindle or improve your relationship

#	Challenge
1	Pray together & set intentions for the month together.
2	Practice listening to one another without interrupting.
3	Make time to talk on the phone instead of texting.
4	Read a book together and exchange thoughts.
5	Recreate your first date.
6	Compliment your partner.
7	Ask your partner what you can do for him/her.
8	Have dinner with no phones allowed at the table.
9	Go for a walk together holding hands.
10	Share your favorite thing about your partner.
11	Bring your partner lunch.
12	Role play.
13	Make plans for church or a spiritual study.
14	Together create your own holiday to celebrate yearly.
15	Take selfies together.
16	Send flirty text messages to each other.
17	Create a scrapbook of all your memories.
18	Surprise your partner with a small gift.
19	Give lots of hugs and kisses.
20	Take on a DIY project for the house.
21	Create a list of long term and short term goals.
22	Learn something new about your partner.
23	Share with one another a personal fanstasy.
24	Write your partner a love letter pouring out your heart.
25	Create a love making playlist.
26	Play a board game together and make a fun bet for whoever wins.
27	Find a yummy recipe and cook it together.
28	Share a bottle of wine with each other over a deep conversation.
29	Reminisce over the good times and share your favorite memory.
30	Never stop doing the little things that make each other happy.

If you walked away from a

toxic,
disloyal,
confusing,
negative,
hurtful,
sad,
abusive,
unhappy,
depressing,
one-sided,
stressful,
low vibrational,
dead-end relationship

YOU WON!

Relationship Goals

BABIES
BEST FRIENDS
COMFORT
DATES
EMPIRE
FOUNDATION
GROWTH
HOME
INFATUATION
INSEPARABLE
LUST
MARRIAGE
PARTNERSHIP
PREGNANCY
PROPERTIES
ROLE PLAY
SOULMATE
TRIPS
VACATIONS

"Men don't have to be perfect to make women happy. All a man really needs to do is to love her like he promised to when they first dated."

- Charles J. Orlando

Nicknames for your other half

```
I F K K B E Q H D H U N R I B M M X L A J X Y J B
G C O S Q W M A N I N B P E J Y R R Q Q J P O K
C U K T N N D O Q G Y U A J I X Q K C U U I C X R
J H R G E D R O S C M U H C H S I I D C R O E Y O
W U V B Y J Q Q X D T E J C O H D N S C R B A Y N
T Z B Y D X T H G I N N I K E Z M G P W I E Z E B
Y B B Q K J Q S F E J A S W E E T Y Y Z U E Q N T
K A Z L S N P U Q F L J H O Z Z E O L Y I P D O I
B B V D I E L E A Q W U R E V O L A O O A V T H B
K F G F E P H N C W Q F S A K G Q A B V V B L D U
L Q F S D M K X E X X O U P A P I C Q O O J E U O D
A U X I W Y Z R V A F Y O N S X O V M S E E D V U
M V X L G Q J S W W U N I M H V V Q S D I B Y N S
A Y O Y J V I M M X J U C M O W W J X P M O D S B
T W K N B D E Z S G R Y E O A V E I D B Q O Q G U
L M K S S E C N I R P R N S M X F V R P S Z M G
I S N R P V X L O K A Q P E D P I Y A X K K H Q C
Y Q Z E G C P C E B W C X B R I F G Q Z S I T O O
H H N Y E N T Q G Y O Y F T X L Q Q Z K I C O E T
U Q O D O U Y E Y D F R B L T T S X K K X D D L A H
R C K P M V Q F K N S G M J H Q D C H B U V L A
B Q D Q O O B Y U N J O Z E U H A Q Z H N T W B D
O A I R F L E Y H Z M I H R O A M J A J T W V I B
Y X H T Z N K O M M O L D X F W A Y C K B G J K Q
V X E Q J W Y R L N S K F I V K K K A A I U S O G
```

BABY
BAE
BEAUTIFUL
BOO
BOOSKI

DADDY
HANDSOME
HONEY
KING
LOVER

MAMI
MUFFIN
MY LOVE
PAPI
PRECIOUS

PRINCESS
QUEEN
SEXY
SWEETY

Ephesians 4:32

Be kind and compassionate to one another, forgiving each other, just as Christ forgave you.

Together lets ...

Check off each activity/plan once completed with partner.

- Read a book
- Finish a puzzle
- Take a dance class
- Start a business
- Set goals
- Make a workout
- Share a secret
- Watch a TV series
- Share a milkshake
- Take a bubble bath
- Go skinny dipping
- Play truth or dare
- Build a fort
- Watch the sunrise
- Take a morning walk
- Take a cooking class
- Go wine tasting
- Go bar hopping
- Carve initials in a tree
- Make a water gun fight
- Save money
- Make love in a random place
- Make a role play
- Go on a road trip
- Try a new local diner
- Tan together
- Learn a new hobby
- Start a family
- Look for a house/an apartment
- Detox
- Get a pedicure
- Get a massage
- Shop for rings
- Get marriage license
- Show public affection
- Visit museum
- Visit zoo
- Go to a theme park
- Vlog a day together
- Try new sex position
- Bake a cake
- Write a love letter to the other
- Go bike riding
- Bachelor's Party
- Go on a mystery date
- Feed the homeless
- Go on a picnic
- Get married!

Baecation Bucket List: World

Check off the places you have been to:

- [ ] Kerry, Ireland
- [ ] Paris, France
- [ ] Dubrovnik, Croatia
- [ ] Edinburgh, Scotland
- [ ] Rome, Italy
- [ ] London, England
- [ ] Amsterdam, Netherlands
- [ ] Copenhagen, Denmark
- [ ] Moscow, Russia
- [ ] Barcelona, Spain
- [ ] Marrakesh, Morocco
- [ ] Cairo, Egypt
- [ ] Kruger National Park, South Africa
- [ ] Cape Town, South Africa
- [ ] Petra, Jordan
- [ ] Dubai, U.A.E.
- [ ] The Maldives
- [ ] Jaipur, India
- [ ] Paro Valley, Bhutan
- [ ] Beijing, China
- [ ] Hong Kong
- [ ] Tokyo, Japan
- [ ] Seoul, Korea
- [ ] Phuket, Thailand
- [ ] Hanoi, Vietnam
- [ ] Bali, Indonesia
- [ ] Singapore
- [ ] Bora Bora, French Polynesia
- [ ] Sydney, Australia
- [ ] Waikato, New Zealand
- [ ] Laucala Island Resort, Fiji
- [ ] Antarctica
- [ ] Vancouver, Canada
- [ ] Barbados
- [ ] Havana, Cuba
- [ ] Machu Picchu, Peru
- [ ] Providencia, Colombia
- [ ] Santiago, Chile
- [ ] Buenos Aires, Argentina
- [ ] Angel Falls, Venezuela

Baecation Bucket List: U.S.A.

Check off the places you have been to:

- ☐ Grand Canyon National Park, Arizona
- ☐ Sedona, Arizona
- ☐ Hawaii
- ☐ Big Sur, California
- ☐ Los Angeles, California
- ☐ Napa Valley, California
- ☐ Austin, Texas
- ☐ Santa Fe, New Mexico
- ☐ Kansas City, Missouri
- ☐ Chicago, Illinois
- ☐ Jackson, Wyoming
- ☐ Indianapolis, Indiana
- ☐ Minneapolis, Minnesota
- ☐ Birmingham, Alabama
- ☐ Livingston, Montana
- ☐ Natchez, Mississippi
- ☐ Phoenix/Scottsdale, Arizona
- ☐ Aspen, Colorado
- ☐ New Orleans, Louisiana
- ☐ Palm Springs, California
- ☐ Philadelphia, Pennsylvania
- ☐ Nantucket, Massachusetts
- ☐ Washington, D.C.
- ☐ New York City, New York
- ☐ Finger Lakes, New York
- ☐ Manchester, Vermont
- ☐ St. Michaels, Maryland
- ☐ Cape Cod, Massachusetts
- ☐ Alaska
- ☐ Columbia River Gorge, Oregon
- ☐ Mount Rushmore, South Dakota
- ☐ Miami, Florida
- ☐ Savannah, Georgia
- ☐ Louisville, Kentucky
- ☐ Newport, Rhode Island
- ☐ Asheville, North Carolina
- ☐ St. Augustine, Florida
- ☐ San Antonio, Texas
- ☐ Charleston, South Carolina
- ☐ Utah National Parks, Utah

Spoil your Partner with:

Love

Loyalty

Respect

Affection

Consistency

Stability

Attention

Time

Encouragement

None of these things are materialistic,
but can improve your relationship
much more than money and material things can.

15 Relationship Affirmations

1. I am overwhelmed with love, happiness and joy.

2. I am loving and lovable.

3. My romantic relationship is healthy, long-lasting and full of love and peace.

4. Every day of my life is filled with love in all areas.

5. The universe blesses me with love every day.

6. I have a loving relationship with myself and others.

7. My relationship grows stronger each day.

8. I give and receive love back with ease and grace.

9. I am safe in my relationship with my partner.

10. My partner and I are a power couple.

11. I have a long-lasting and fulfilling relationship.

12. I am in a wonderful relationship with someone who treats me right.

13. My partner is my soulmate.

14. I am surrounded by love.

15. My partner appreciates me for me.

50 Ways
to spice up your relationship!

1. Surprise her with a bouquet of flowers (just because)
2. Bring him lunch to his job in a trench coat wearing something sexy or nothing underneath.
3. Cook a meal in lingerie and serve it to him.
4. Grab your partner unexpected and passionately make out with them for a minute straight.
5. Try a new sex position.
6. Visit a sex store and pick out some items you each would like to try.
7. Flirt in public with each other.
8. Send sexy text messages to each other throughout the day to build anticipation.
9. Surprise her or him with a spa date.
10. Enjoy a candle light dinner.
11. Go out and share a dessert together and feed it to one another.
12. After enjoying a night out together ... once you arrive at home make love in the car before getting out.
13. Go skinny dipping together.
14. Play a truth or dare game.
15. Play a drinking game together. (Ex. beer pong, never have I ever, flip cup)
16. Make time for morning sex.
17. Take turns photographing each other.
18. Take a shower together ... have sex in the shower.
19. Rent a hotel and get away for the weekend.
20. Spend the day together without phones and no tv.
21. Turn on slow music together and dance.
22. Buy each other a random gift.
23. Create a date-night jar, add different ideas for dates in the jar, every week choose a date.
24. Take a sip and paint class together.
25. Bar hop and show lots of public affection.

50 Ways

to spice up your relationship!

26. Tease your man while he is at work and send him seductive messages.	**27.** Make a list of reasons why you love each other and share them with each other.	**28.** Go on a double date with friends.	**29.** Take yearly anniversary vacations.	**30.** Be spontaneous.
31. Make time for morning sex.	**32.** Take turns photographing each other.	**33.** Leave a note in red lipstick on the mirror for him to wake up to.	**34.** ???	**35.** Cuddle on the couch and watch a romantic movie together.
36. Constantly compliment each other.	**37.** Say I love you multiple times throughout the day. (If you truly love them)	**38.** Take a rose petal bubble bath together with a glass of champagne.	**39.** Stay up late talking and expressing your feelings to one another.	**40.** Do a lap dance or striptease for each other.
41. Play wrestle with each other ... this could lead to hot unexpected sex.	**42.** Tell jokes and make each other laugh.	**43.** Before bed pray together and don't go to bed upset at each other.	**44.** Read a sex book together to learn new tricks.	**45.** Sleep naked together.
46. Do something that you did early in your relationship that your partner liked.	**47.** Make bets that lead to pleasure for whoever wins the bet.	**48.** Learn how to say something sexy in a different language.	**49.** Change the scenery in the room to make it more appealing.	**50.** Always be open and honest, do things out of love, be positive and happy.

Gift Ideas for HIM and HER

Him

- Tickets to his favorite game.
- A nice wallet or briefcase
- New electronic gadget
- A good tool box
- A nice pair of shoes
- A personalized cigar set
- A nice meaningful card
- A nice watch
- His favorite video game
- Some good reading books
- Golf/tennis lessons
- Concert tickets
- A nice get-away
- A personalized bible
- A nice cologne
- A personalized flask
- A BBQ grill set
- Whiskey/wine decanter
- A nice jacket/belt
- Sportswear/ underwear
- A basket with his favorite snacks

Her

- Edible arrangements
- Balloons and flowers
- Jewelry
- Her favorite candy
- Lingerie/robe/pajamas
- A perfume Set
- Gift cards/money
- Makeup/ lipgloss
- Candles
- A nice purse
- A cute outfit
- Pampering/spa date
- Coffee/tea mug
- Leggings
- Hair tools
- A planner/journal
- A camera
- A good reading book
- Skin care essentials
- A phone case
- A nice pair of shoes/heels
- Dinner dates
- Bath bombs

The best gifts are always the ones you least expect. Take the time to put a smile on your boyfriend´s/girlfriend´s face... it will go a long way.

Qualities of my Partner

I value my partner because:

My partner makes me happy by:

What I like most about my partner:

Best memories with my partner:

The qualities I am attracted to most are:

Frugal Date Ideas

No matter how long you have been together... always make quality time for one another whether you are on a budget or have a little money to spend. It's the thought that counts. Check out some recommendations below.

FREE

- Walk downtown
- Have a picnic
- Go bike riding/hiking
- Go fishing
- Visit the library
- Do some window shopping
- Go to the beach
- Do some volunteer/charity work

Under $20

- Go on an ice cream date
- Go Bowling
- Have a movie date
- Have a skating date
- Visit a karaoke bar
- Take a fitness/dance class
- Visit an Arcade
- drink a Happy Hour cocktail

Under $50

- Go on lunch date
- Go wine tasting
- Take a paint class
- Play laser tag
- Play paint ball
- Do zip lining
- Go horseback riding
- Visit a comedy show

Under $100

- Go on a dinner date
- Have a couples massage
- Visit a local concert
- Go golfing
- Rent a jet ski
- Visit a sports event
- Take a cooking class
- Go kart racing

At home

- Watch Netflix & chill
- Play board games
- Cook dinner together
- Dance slowly
- Bake a cake
- Do a puzzle

With kids

- Color/draw/paint
- Go camping/Make a bonfire
- Visit a zoo or farm
- Visit a pool/waterpark
- Do outside sports
- Build a fort

Search for Words that "EVERY RELATIONSHIP NEEDS ..."

```
            F C Z F                    W L T Z
          A I C X J A                G O L P R M
        X T N Q B N M I            Q V H L I P U M
      P B T M Y P X U G T D E G D D H Q W S N
    Y N S R E K X W J H D H E A O Y S U N Y T J
  W L R C A Y F E N N N O I N U G C D X S H H M S
  S Y O G C O M M U N I C A T I O N N R N Y A V F
  E H M H T J I C G C W R P Q K F S E E L T P U E
  A C A O I S F D J O F H M U L N T I H X I P C D
  S V N N O N O P H M I D F A S E C R U B L I Z O
  L G C E N M X Q T P N R Y L A S L F U Z I N O N
    S E S I J O G G R T H C I C T X F V L B E O
    V V T Y T J L N O I O L T R M C I W O A S W
      C Y H I A X E M M F O Y I P E E H F T S
        G O C S P R I A A N T F Y H B I U S
        H B Y X T S C M G I I H R C X H
          T E L S I Y I E M C K G U A
            G A V N U L V E I G S O
              O V G E Y I W N V Z
                C V F A T R G C
                  N B D Y D P
                    Y T N A
                      K V
```

ATTRACTION	FRIENDSHIP	LONGEVITY	SACRIFICING
COMMUNICATION	GOD	LOVE	STABILITY
COMPROMISING	HAPPINESS	PATIENCE	STRENGTH
FAITH	HONESTY	QUALITY TIME	TRUST
FAMILY	INTIMACY	ROMANCE	UNION

Real couples struggle together, plot together, hustle together, and shine together.

Love can be very complicated, confusing and can feel like a never ending maze. But through out all the curves, turns, ups and downs... you have to fight to the end.

Key: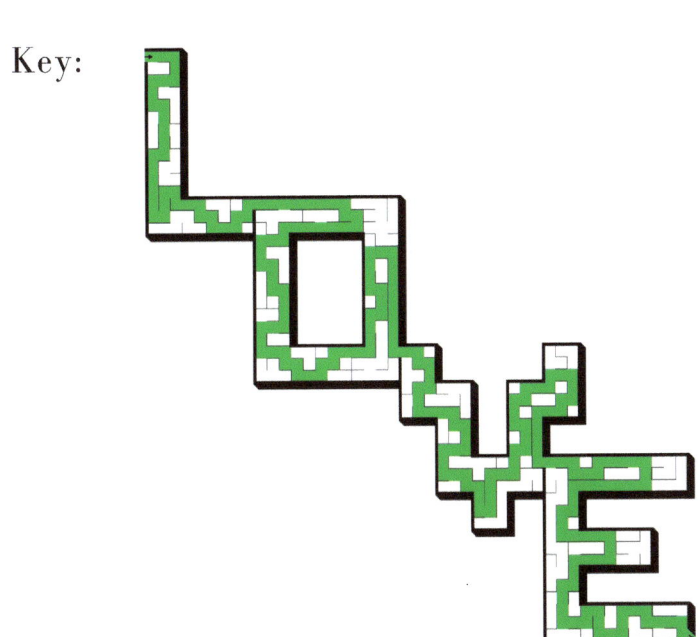

Never cheat on someone you don't want to lose, for someone you don't want to keep.

Relationship Quiz Time!

On a separate sheet of paper answer the following questions about your partner. Before completing the exercise be sure to create an answer key so you can grade this quiz fairly. The loser has to take the winner on a date. Good luck!

1. What is my favorite food?
2. Where was I born?
3. Where was our first date?
4. What is my favorite hobby?
5. What is my favorite candy?
6. What is our anniversary date?
7. What is my dream job?
8. What is my favorite movie?
9. Who is my favorite singer/artist?
10. Who is/are my best friend/s?
11. What turns me on?
12. What is my favorite sex position?
13. What is my biggest goal right now?
14. What is my dream car?
15. What is my favorite sports team?
16. What is my favorite color?
17. What is my biggest pet peeve?
18. What is my favorite animal?
19. What food do I hate the most?
20. What is my favorite TV show/ series?
21. What is my biggest passion?
22. What is my favorite snack?
23. What do I buy more than anything else?
24. What attribute do I love most about myself?
25. How many kids do I want?

This is a fun exercise to get to know your partner better.
Read the answers out loud and don't get butthurt over who knows least.
It's all fun and games.

25 Ways to romance your man!

Use these ideas to connect with your husband/ boyfriend and show him appreciation

1. Pray for God's help.
2. Cook his favorite meal.
3. Express your love through action & words.
4. Always kiss him goodbye and greet him with a big warm hug.
5. Help him with an activity unexpectedly.
6. Take interest in his hobbies.
7. Give eye contact when he speaks.
8. Ask him about his day while giving him a massage.
9. Write him a love note and put it in his wallet or on his car.
10. Apologize when you're wrong and tell him when he is right.
11. Let go of small annoyances and don't nag about petty things.
12. Love him **unconditionally**!
13. Uplift him when he is going through something or feeling down.
14. Keep it sexy! Wear something nice to bed here and there.
15. Be a little more aggressive in the bedroom. (Initiate sex)
16. Give a soft answer and avoid raising your voice.
17. Sit on his lap and show him affection.
18. Play a nice love song and dedicate it to him.
19. Buy him a random gift.
20. Brag about him and boost his confidence.
21. Acknowledge when he tries and thank him.
22. Be the one to take him on date that he doesn't expect.
23. Laugh at his jokes, compliment him, encourage him.
24. Feel on his muscles and his body.
25. Tell him how proud he makes you.

"If a man wants you, nothing can keep him away.
If he doesn't want you, nothing can make him stay."
- *Oprah Winfrey*

Romans 12:10

Be devoted to one another in love. Honor one another above yourselves.

A successful relationship requires falling in love over and over again with the same person.

10 Ways to Support One Another in a Relationship

1 *Ask them how they're feeling and actually listen.*

2 *Look for ways to put a smile on your partners face randomly. Random surprises always keep the relationship in a good space. A simple note on the mirror or a single rose can go a long way.*

3 *Talk about your deep rooted issues. If your partner is not being themselves, help them understand you're there for them and by their side. Depression is real and sometimes one may not realize they're going through it.*

4 *Support their dreams and goals. Always encourage them and show them you believe in them. Sometimes just that one person cheating them on can give them the extra push that they need.*

5 *Always remind them that you love them and speak positively when talking to them.*

6 *Check on them throughout the day or week, depending on the the status or depth of your relationship.*

7 *Compromise. Everything isn't always about you. Sometimes you have to put your partner before you. Relationships are give and take and shouldn't be one sided.*

8 *Offer help when you see that they're in need. Not everyone likes to ask, so offering a helping hand can really go a long way and show your partner that you truly care.*

9 *Make it clear to your partner that you're a team. When you're building a relationship with someone, you're in it together, not separately. Don't compete with one another but compete together.*

10 *Speak highly of one another to each other and to others. Focus on the good and avoid giving attention to anything negative. Let go of the petty situations, they're a complete waist of time that you could be spending loving on each other.*

5 Love Languages

Act of Service

Can I give you a foot massage?

Quality Time

Would you like to go see a movie?

Words of Affirmation

I love being in your company.

Physical Touch

Hugs, kisses and intimacy.

Gifts

I bought you those shoes you liked.

Resolutions for Arguments

10 Healthy tips to help solve conflicts in a relationship.

#1 — *Speak and respond in a respectful calm manner.*

#2 — *Listen to understand one another and not to respond.*

#3 — *Walk away if you feel like you're going to lose your temper.*

#4 — *Respect each other's personal space. Keep your hands to yourself.*

#5 — *Pray together on the situation. Avoid going to bed with your issues still on your heart and mind.*

Resolutions for Arguments

10 Healthy tips to help solve conflicts in a relationship.

#6 *Take some time before responding off of your heated emotions.*

#7 *Apologize when you're in the wrong and take accountability for your actions.*

#8 *Do not hold onto grudges if you accept your partner's apology.*

#9 *Do not bring up past issues for current problems. Let the past be the past.*

#10 *Seek counseling or spiritual help by an unbiased professional. Be open to truly getting to the bottom of the issue and coming to a resolution.*

Couples that pray together stay together.

My Relationship Prayer

Open prompt to write your prayer for what you're seeking.

It is important to respect differences in how we all give and receive love. Most of us tend to love others the same way we want to be loved but this doesn't work when you have different love languages. Therefore, increasing your awareness and respect of diversity of love languages is an important first step.

- Dr. Wyatt Fisher

"A wise woman knows the importance of speaking life into her man. If you love him: believe in him, encourage him & be his peace."

- Denzel Washington

DISTANCE

can never separate

TWO HEARTS

that are meant to be!

Dream Wedding

Use this page to describe your ideal wedding:

E.g. Where would it be? Who would you invite? Would it be a big or intimate, small wedding? What would the scenery be? What colors would you choose? Etc. ...

_____
_____
_____
_____
_____
_____
_____
_____
_____
_____
_____
_____
_____
_____
_____

Wedding Checklist!

A short guide for planning your big day.

- ○ Start a wedding book/binder
- ○ Decide on date with partner
- ○ Choose a location
- ○ Decide on budget
- ○ Choose wedding party
- ○ Decide on number of guests
- ○ Search for venues
- ○ Choose a wedding theme/color
- ○ Choose a dress shop
- ○ Send invitations 12 months ahead
- ○ Send email reminder with date
- ○ Finalize guest RSVPS
- ○ Register for gifts
- ○ Book a florist
- ○ Choose bridesmaids' dresses
- ○ Choose groomsmen attire
- ○ Choose tuxedo
- ○ Decide wedding cake & flavor
- ○ Choose a caterer
- ○ Food taste/cake test
- ○ Book honeymoon
- ○ Make hotel/flight arrangements
- ○ Order wedding favors
- ○ Shop for wedding decor/accessories

- ○ Organize a Bridal shower
- ○ Plan Bachelorette party
- ○ Plan Bachelor party
- ○ Make sure rings fit
- ○ Choose reception venue
- ○ Arrange seating by names
- ○ Meet with your officiant
- ○ Book rehearsal dinner
- ○ Finalize reception menu
- ○ Order gifts for bridal party
- ○ Pick up marriage license
- ○ Professional hairstylist
- ○ Professional makeup artist
- ○ Attend final dress/tux fitting
- ○ Practice/create a first dance
- ○ Hire a DJ & photographer
- ○ Pay for all services
- ○ Order thank you cards
- ○ Attend a marriage class
- ○ Speak with a pastor as a couple
- ○ Buy your groom a wedding gift
- ○ Buy your bride a wedding gift
- ○ Pray a lot!!!
- ○ Say I do!

Mark 10:9

Let no man separate what God has joined together.

Weddings Savings

Write down your saving goals and color the check circle when you have achieved your goal.

Amount Goal:

Budget/Saving Guide for House

Write down your saving goals and color the house when you have achieved your goal.

Amount Goal:

Every Relationship goes through Tribulations

```
W Y T N I A T R E C N U S N T D M F Y R P O W Y T
L M S W B V L W W I E F O E I S T R U G G L E S C
X H P Y E W W D S N I I K S G T N D H R D O P J O
S K T B I A I S R G T F A Z T N S T U G S M R T N
K U T S G S E U H A K G E X S Q E K K T H K W K F
C L V D T N F T R H R V R C Q I D L W K Z I B R L
A V F A K P S A N E V K B O L X K A L X G S L V I
B E N C B E P K E I F U T X B I S E K A T S I M C
T C I T L E K M N R A E R V S T F C T F H K F U T
E S L A S M E T I D B P A B K P B M D T W C O N Y
S P Q T J N I S T N Q R E O R F S I Y Y V I L L R
X J S C T H P D I S C M H V Z E N W E N H P U M L
E I M S T L C N U L A M H E M U A O W B J E B N Y
W B J B R L E C I N E G G B C M V K Q K N Z R H F
H A Q C A R D M M R E N L S M K D H U E E S C D X
T W W D A G C J S I V O C N M B G U S P E E K U J
Q G W Q P D A A E Q C I W E C E O L B Y S U Q C D
L F E Z F J P C T K R R Y B D D L H F N S O R K N
Y K Y X Z X T W V H Y Y V A V M T A B W S H W J I H
L A H S P S F L D S S E R T S B K Z O T S X L S Z
E T W O J K L L O Z Z O Y G Y F P J S R R D N E Y X
U T G B H K W S U K N T P G S B F Z C O P A R P O
B A P V N U W F B Y C S Y J G G P X L F C O M S D
T R O U B L E S T A N L R G K C V T G X X L V O S
O V N G E X D I S J C L X H R C F Z Y I L T P O L
```

BREKUPS	DOUBTS	PROBLEMS	STRESS
CHALLENGES	FIGHTS	SEPARATION	STRUGGLES
CONFLICTS	HEARTBREAK	SETBACKS	TROUBLES
DISAGREEMENTS	MISTAKES	SICKNESS	UNCERTAINTY
DISTANCE	PAIN	SILENCE	

If you are hurting, you should be healing ... not dating.

15 Signs

You are dating a narcissist

1. They lack empathy, compassion and feelings for others.

2. Narcissist have a strong sense of entitlement. They feel as though they are better than others and are always right.

3. They're hypocrites and pretend to have morals and values that they don't truly possess.

4. They have expectations of others that they don't practice themselves and they never take accountability.

5. Narcissist will tear you down even when they're in the wrong. When they hurt you, they will make you feel at fault and guilty for something that they did.

6. They believe that they have the right to mistreat you and hurt you, but you don't have the right to react or stand up for yourself.

7. They are soul crushers and come across as cold and heartless.

8. They are never there when you need them but will expect you to be there for them through everything.

9. They will manipulate you, control you, abuse you and try to isolate you.

10. They tend to apologize and beg for forgiveness when they think you're going to leave them. But they will make the same mistakes again once you forgive them.

11. They lie, cheat, steal and tend to have addictions.

12. They will drain the life out of you and make you lose yourself trying to please them. Nothing will ever completely please them.

13. Narcissists are always the VICTIMS!

14. They are very impulsive and get bored easily.

15. They have really bad anger problems and will throw a tantrum and not let you speak.

If you're dating anyone with 3 or more of these characteristics ... RUN, very FAST! This type of person is very ruined and will ruin you throughout the entire relationship. There is nothing cute about a TOXIC relationship. Get help and leave.

You deserve a relationship with someone who will never have you second guessing or thinking about where you stand with them.

Healthy vs Toxic Relationships

Healthy

- Puts God first
- Has honesty & trust
- Listens to one another
- Shows compassion
- Forgives
- Communicates openly
- Is willing to compromise
- Respects each other
- Admits mistakes
- Shows unconditional love
- Takes accountability
- Supports each other
- Space and boundaries
- Friendship & fun
- Happiness & laughter
- Pleasure & intimacy
- Individual high self-esteem
- Expresses feelings
- Give and receive
- Sacrifice
- Growth & improvement

Toxic

- Plays mind games
- Constant lies/ no trust
- Tries to change you
- Shows no care or emotion
- Holds grudges/ unforgiving
- Argues and yell
- Doesn't commit
- Rude and disrespectful
- Make excuses
- Shows no affection or love
- Doesn't take responsibility
- Lacks support
- Clingy and controlling
- Never likes to do anything
- Always angry, sad, or mad
- Lack of pleasure
- Low self esteem
- Keeps emotions inside
- Take and never give
- Selfish and painful
- Shows no growth

Be with the person that brings out the best in you. No one is perfect but there will be someone that is perfect for you.

Don't ask why someone keeps hurting you. Ask yourself why you keep letting them.

SITUATONSHIPS

Let us just hang out almost everyday,
go out to places with one another,
have sex often,
tell each other we love one another,
and be confused on the fact
that we are not officially together
even though we act like we are.

Don't feel bad for knowing you deserve better.

Try to escape the ...

Don't let them put your through hell and call it love. Love doesn't hurt and love doesn't leave you feeling worthless.
Let go, and move on!

15 Signs

You are in a domestic violence relationship

Domestic Violence is at an all time high and is nothing to take lightly. It can consist of physical, mental, emotional, psychological, sexual and even financial abuse. All abuse includes some kind of willful harm against a partner; male or female. ABUSE IS NEVER OKAY!

1. Any physical pain being afflicted upon you is abuse: hitting, punching, slapping, kicking, scratching, choking or spitting.

2. Unpredictable and intimidating behavior.

3. They're hypocrites and pretend to have morals and values that they don't truly possess.

4. They have expectations of others that they don't practice themselves and they never take accountability.

5. Narcissist will tear you down even when they're in the wrong. When they hurt you, they will make you feel at fault and guilty for something that they did.

6. They believe that they have the right to mistreat you and hurt you, but you don't have the right to react or stand up for yourself.

7. They are soul crushers and come across as cold and heartless.

8. They are never there when you need them but will expect you to be there for them through everything.

9. They will manipulate you, control you, abuse you and try to isolate you.

10. They tend to apologize and beg for forgiveness when they think you're going to leave them. But they will make the same mistakes again once you forgive them.

11. They lie, cheat, steal and tend to have addictions.

12. They will drain the life out of you and make you lose yourself trying to please them. Nothing will ever completely please them.

13. Narcissists are always the VICTIMS!

14. They are very impulsive and get bored easily.

15. They have really bad anger problems and will throw a tantrum and not let you speak

If you are going through any type of domestic abuse, please get help.
The national domestic abuse hotline is available 24/7/365:
1-800-799-7233 | 1-800-787-3224 (TTY) | En Espanol

Weigh out the Good and the Bad

PROS	CONS
List the good	List the bad

No relationship is perfect but sometimes you have to take a step back, weigh out the good and the bad to see if it is worth continuing or letting go...

"Stay away from people who can't take responsibility for their actions and who make you feel bad for being angry at them when they do you wrong."

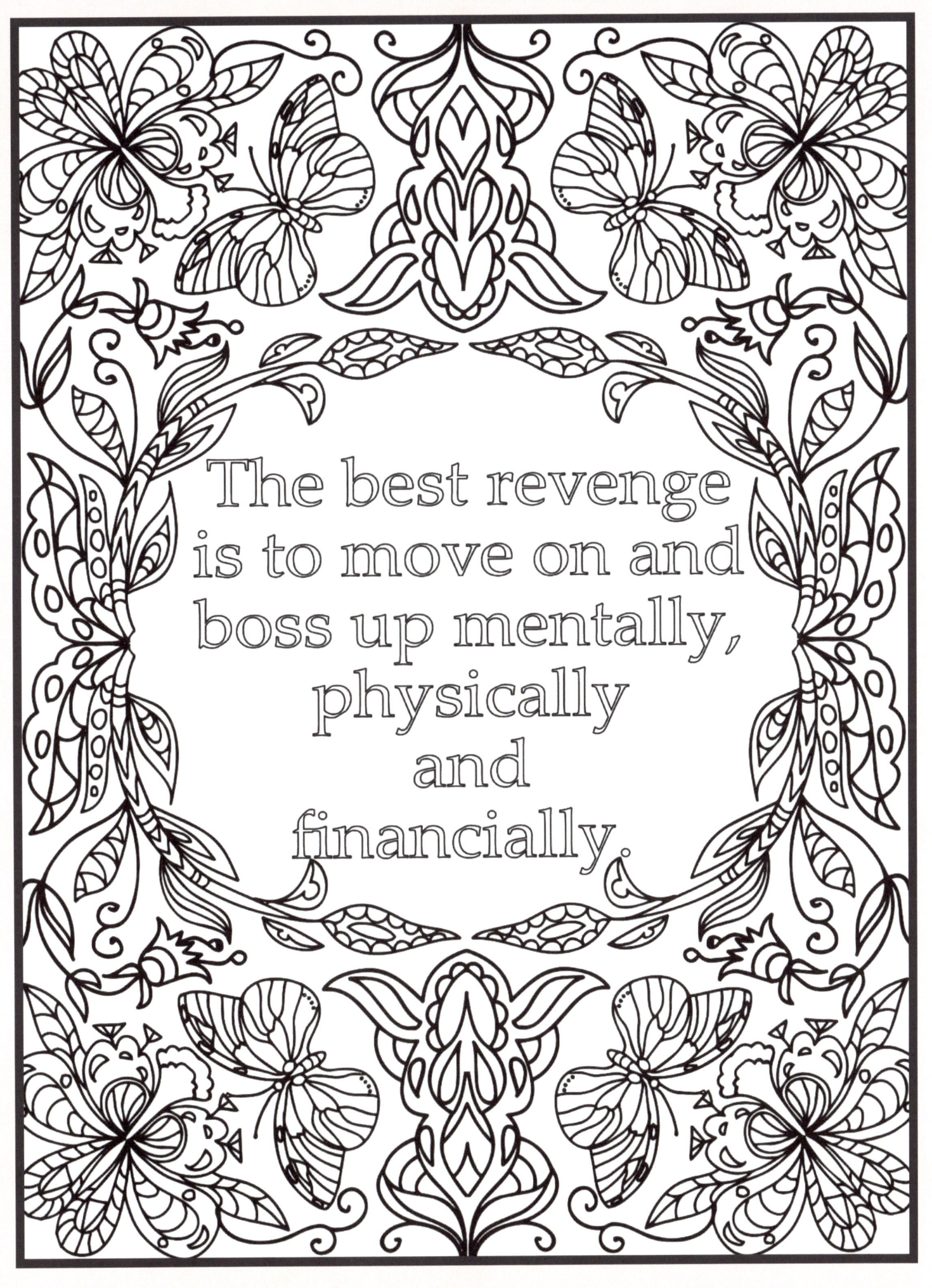

Turn Pain into Growth

Have you ever experienced a heartbreak? Explain your biggest heartbreak and how you were able to move past it. What did you learn the most from this painful experience?

_____
_____
_____
_____
_____
_____
_____
_____
_____
_____
_____
_____
_____
_____
_____
_____
_____
_____
_____
_____

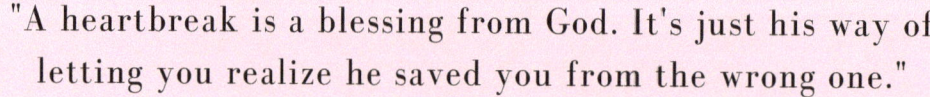 

"A heartbreak is a blessing from God. It's just his way of letting you realize he saved you from the wrong one."

Life is too short to be waiting on somebody to act right.

Express your feelings

Express your feelings

Express your feelings

Express your feelings

Express your feelings

Express your feelings

Express your feelings

Express your feelings

Express your feelings

Express your feelings

AFTER ALL,
SOULMATES ALWAYS
END UP TOGETHER

For more books and merch from me, please visit.

www. thebombchellelife.com

Get In Touch

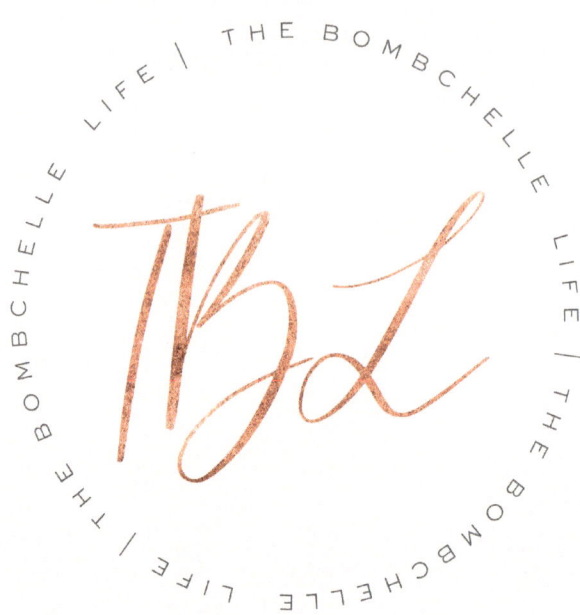

Thank you so much for your love and support.
Be sure to follow us on social media for new releases, sneak peeks and giveaways.

The Bombchelle Life

@thebombchellelife
@bombchellebabes

Suscribe to my channel
THE BOMBCHELLE LIFE

Email us at
thebombchellelife@gmail.com

www.ingramcontent.com/pod-product-compliance
Lightning Source LLC
Chambersburg PA
CBHW041544220426
43665CB00002B/31